Contents

CHAPTER 1

Fan Frenzy

Cameras flash. TV reporters shout questions. Loudest of all is the chanting of excited fans. Hundreds of them crowd around the red carpet, waving homemade signs and holding mobile phone cameras in the air. Some have camped out for days to get a good spot. It is a once-in-a-lifetime chance to see their big screen idols. For Robert Pattinson, it is another working day at a film **premiere**.

Robert steps out of his limo, and the crowd erupt into a chorus of screams and cries. He smiles and stops to sign everything from books, to pizza boxes. Some fans have bizarre requests, such as asking him to bite them! They are thinking of Robert in his most famous role – the vampire Edward Cullen in the *Twilight Saga*. Robert is known for his good humour. He takes it all in his stride.

Finally, Robert stops to be interviewed by reporters from around the world. They want to know about his latest film, his designer clothes, and even his love life. Robert has to shout his answers above the noise of the fan frenzy.

premiere the first public showing of a film

Robert Pattinson

by Jennifer M. Besel

www.raintreepublishers.co.uk
Visit our website to find out
more information about
Raintree books.

To order:
☎ Phone 0845 6044371
🖷 Fax +44 (0) 1865 312263
🖳 Email myorders@raintreepublishers.co.uk

Customers from outside the UK please telephone +44 1865 312262

Raintree is an imprint of Capstone Global Library Limited, a company incorporated in England and Wales having its registered office at 7 Pilgrim Street, London, EC4V 6LB – Registered company number: 6695582

Editors: Megan Peterson and John-Paul Wilkins
Designer: Joanna Hinton-Malivoire
Media Researchers: Marcie Spence and Tracy Cummins
Production Specialist: Eirian Griffiths
Originated by Capstone Global Library Ltd
Printed and bound in China by Leo Paper Products Ltd

ISBN 978 1 406 22951 6 (paperback)
15 14 13 12 11
10 9 8 7 6 5 4 3 2 1

British Library Cataloguing in Publication Data
Besel, Jennifer M.
Robert Pattinson. – (Star biographies)
791.4'3'028'092-dc22
A full catalogue record for this book is available from the British Library.

Acknowledgements
Alamy/Allstar Picture Library, 18; AP Images/Tammie Arroyo, 7; Corbis/Steven Georges/Press-Telegram, 25; Courtesy of How To Films Ltd., 13; Courtesy of Tower House Preparatory School, 10; Getty Images/ Christopher Polk, 27; Getty Images/Franco S. Origlia, 21; Getty Images/Jeff Kravitz/FilmMagic, 6; Getty Images/Jon Furniss/WireImage, cover; Getty Images/Jordan Strauss/Wire Image, 5; Getty Images /Mark Sullivan/Wire Image, 29; Newscom, 16; Newscom/Murray Close/Warner Bros. Pictures, 17; Newscom/Summit Entertainment/MCT, 23; Supplied by Capital Pictures/Steve Finn, 9; Tandem Productions/VIP Medienfonds 2&3 Courtesy of Sony Pictures Home Entertainment, 15.

We would like to thank Isabel Thomas for her invaluable help in the preparation of this book.

Some words appear in bold, **like this**. They are explained at the bottom of the page, or in the glossary.

Robert had trouble speaking over the screaming fans at the *Eclipse* premiere in Los Angeles, USA.

"This is my life. People know my name and ambush me in public and try to figure out what hotel I'm staying at and ask me to bite them and want to touch my hair. I have accepted it as real now, but it still feels surreal."

Robert at the premiere of the first Twilight film, in 2008

In demand

Gradually, the stars disappear inside for the film screening. The red carpet is empty, but the fans continue to cheer for Robert long into the night. It's easy to see why he often tops polls of Hollywood's most important people.

After the screening there is a party. Robert is in demand again. Hollywood filmmakers introduce themselves. They want him to be in their films. A-list celebrities wander over to say hello. Robert is one of the most popular young actors in the world. It is a far cry from his **rebellious** childhood growing up in London.

Robert is very close to his Twilight Saga co-stars Kristen Stewart and Taylor Lautner.

rebellious struggling against the people in charge

Fans love Robert's wild Twilight hairstyle.

"People are scared of my hair. But it starts washing itself after about three weeks. I'm just saying that. But, yeah, if it doesn't look dirty, why wash it?"

Robert talks about his famous hair in an interview with USA Today

Star Facts

Full name:
Robert Thomas Pattinson

Date of birth:
13 May 1986

Nicknames: Rob, R-Patz, Patty

Favourite sports: Football, skiing, snowboarding

Trademark: Scruffy hair

Pets: When his dog Patty died, Robert described it as the worst day of his life. In 2011, he adopted a puppy from a rescue shelter to keep him company as he travels the world.

Favourite musicians:
Van Morrison, Jimi Hendrix

Favourite author: Martin Amis

Drives: lost his car in LA after forgetting where he parked it; now has a private chauffeur

Lives: London, UK and Los Angeles, USA

In his fridge: Peach Snapple soft drink and Pepperoni hot pockets

CHAPTER 2

Growing up in London

Robert grew up in Barnes, a **suburb** of London. Robert's dad Richard sold **vintage** cars, and his mum Clare worked for a modelling agency. Robert is the youngest of their three children. His older sisters, Elizabeth and Victoria, liked to tease him. Robert had a good sense of humour. He even let them dress him up as a girl and call him Claudia! Robert's family life shaped his easy-going, fun personality.

Robert had a comfortable but ordinary childhood. He even delivered newspapers to earn spending money. Robert jokes that his £10 per week wage made him obsessed with money. Little did he know that he would be a multi-millionnaire by his early twenties!

"I quite liked ... a cartoon with rapper MC Hammer in it – Hammertime – I loved that cartoon, it was genius! They don't make cartoons like that anymore."

Robert speaking to *CBBC Newsround* about his childhood

When he was younger, Robert enjoyed playing music and acting in school plays.

Robert's first school was an all-boys' prep school.

Breaking the rules

As a young boy, Robert attended the Tower House Preparatory School in London. He did not focus on work, and became known as a bit of a troublemaker. Once he was made lunch monitor. Instead of making sure other pupils obeyed the rules, Robert jokes that he stole his classmates' chips. He even won an 'untidy desk award'! When Robert was 12, he was expelled from Tower House. He has never revealed what caused the trouble.

At the age of 13, Robert began attending the Harrodian School in London. Drama was a big part of student life, with special studios for rehearsing plays. Robert also got to enjoy the school's heated swimming pool, state-of-the-art science labs, and music centre.

Early passions

Robert admits that he was not keen on schoolwork. But there were two things that he did work hard at – music and drama. Robert started playing the piano when he was just four years old. He took up his second instrument, classical guitar, when he was five.

Drama was an activity that Robert enjoyed at school. He acted in several school plays from the age of six, including *Lord of the Flies*. At that stage he wasn't thinking about an acting career. He dreamed of being a musician. By the age of 14, Robert was in a rap trio. His hero was superstar rapper Eminem.

Reluctant star

Robert resisted becoming an actor. But his father watched him in school plays. He saw that Robert had a special talent. He wanted his son to be an actor, and he was very vocal about it. He encouraged Robert to join a small acting club near their home. Robert refused, but his father kept pushing. Robert went to work at the Barnes Theatre Company when he was 15. He helped out backstage, organizing **props** and moving **sets**.

After working on his first show, Robert decided to give acting a try. He **auditioned** for a role in the musical *Guys and Dolls*. To his surprise, he landed the role of a Cuban dancer. Robert found himself becoming a regular in the Barnes Theatre Group. He won the roles of George Gibbs in *Our Town*, and Lord Evelyn Oakleigh in *Anything Goes*. After Robert's performance as Alec in *Tess of the d'Urbervilles*, he was approached by an **agent**. The agent convinced Robert to begin his acting career.

"I play a lot of music. That's what I wanted to do before the acting thing accidentally took off – be a musician."

Robert in an interview with *Vanity Fair Magazine*

audition to try out for a role

agent someone who helps actors to find work

Robert has been able to use his musical talents in some of his films.

A musical back-up plan

Music is a big part of Robert's life. He is a talented guitar and piano player. His guitar goes everywhere with him, keeping him company when he is far from friends and family.

Robert and three of his friends play gigs from time to time. They aren't looking for a record deal – they play their rocky-blues style music for fun. Along with his friends, Robert also writes original music. Two of their songs, "Never Think" and "Let Me Sign" are on the *Twilight* **soundtrack**. Robert also performs three of his own songs on the soundtrack to his 2008 film, *How to Be*.

Sometimes Robert performs at open mic nights in pubs and clubs. When he plays solo, Robert calls himself Bobby Dupea. This is the name of a character played by Robert's favourite actor, Jack Nicholson, in the film *Five Easy Pieces*. Robert has said that music is his backup plan if acting fails. He would love to set up a company that produces new music, films and writing.

CHAPTER 3

Bitten by the acting bug

Acting at the Barnes Theatre Company opened many doors for Robert. At the age of 17, he was able to make the leap from stage to screen. Robert played the role of Giselher in the **epic** adventure *Ring of the Nibelungs* (2004). This made-for-TV film gave Robert his first taste of working in front of a camera. He lived in his own apartment for three months while filming in Cape Town, South Africa.

Next, Robert was cast in a minor role in his first big film, *Vanity Fair* (2004). He even got the chance to work with Oscar-winning actor Reese Witherspoon. Robert proudly attended the film's red-carpet **premiere**. But then came disappointment. As he watched the film for the first time, Robert realized that his scenes had been cut. No one had even told him.

Robert rebounded with a role in a play called *The Woman Before*, at London's Royal Court Theatre. But just one week before opening night, Robert was fired for "trying to take risks" with his acting. He learned that an actor's luck can change quickly.

Aged 17, Robert (far left) starred in the TV film *Ring of the Nibelungs*.

Becoming a star

Disappointment didn't last long for Robert. The casting **agent** from *Vanity Fair* invited him to try out for the fourth *Harry Potter* film. After just two **auditions**, Robert was offered the role of quidditch player Cedric Diggory. He filmed his action-packed part for 11 months. Robert enjoyed performing stunts with his co-star Daniel Radcliffe, who played Harry. In one scene, Cedric and Harry chase each other through a maze of magical, moving hedges. Robert didn't mind the bruises left by the motorized hedges. He even spent three weeks learning how to scuba dive for the role. Robert kept a journal and wrote about his experiences. He also wrote about his fear of never landing another part.

Robert had fun filming scenes with Harry Potter co-star Daniel Radcliffe.

In November 2005, *Harry Potter and the Goblet of Fire* opened to excited audiences worldwide. Playing Cedric Diggory was a huge boost for Robert's acting career. Film reviews praised his performance.

"The day before [the Goblet of Fire London premiere] I was just sitting in Leicester Square, happily being ignored by everyone. Then suddenly strangers are screaming your name. Amazing."

Robert in an interview with Vanity Fair magazine

While filming, Robert performed many of his own stunts.

Robert was both excited and nervous at the London premiere of *Harry Potter and the Goblet of Fire*.

New opportunities

Robert's success in *Harry Potter* gave him a greater choice of roles. He landed parts in two made-for-TV films, including *The Bad Mother's Handbook* in which he starred alongside Catherine Tate. He also appeared in a flashback scene in the 2007 blockbuster, *Harry Potter and the Order of the Phoenix*.

In 2008, Robert proved that he was a good comedy actor in the British film *How to Be*. He played Art, a 20-year-old man who moves back in with his parents. With the assistance of a self-help guide, Art explores his life. Robert's performance earned him the Best Actor Award at the 2008 Strasbourg International Film Festival in France.

Robert also took on the part of famous artist Salvador Dali in the film *Little Ashes*. To prepare for the role, he read every biography of Dali he could find. *Little Ashes* **premiered** at London's Raindance Film Festival in October 2008. But both parts were about to be overshadowed by the film that would make Robert Pattinson a household name.

"Harry Potter was what made me become an actor. I credit Harry Potter with everything else that's come since for me."
Robert from an interview with MTV

CHAPTER 4

The role of a lifetime

As Robert worked on the Harry Potter films, a new series of books was taking the world by storm. *Twilight* and its sequels, written by Stephenie Meyer, became a global hit. Teenage girls adored the central male character, a beautiful vampire called Edward Cullen. When Summit Entertainment decided to turn *Twilight* into a film, fans demanded that director Catherine Hardwicke cast the right person to play Edward. She had more than 3,000 actors to choose from!

Catherine almost passed up Robert for the part. She had seen a photograph of him, but she wasn't impressed. Not really believing he could get the role, Robert flew to California, for an auditon at Catherine's home. He had to perform a love scene with Kristen Stewart, who had already been cast to play Bella Swan. That night, Catherine saw something in Robert that his photo had not revealed. She had found the actor who could pull off the intense vampire character at the heart of Stephanie's book.

Robert wanted to work with Kristen from the moment he met her.

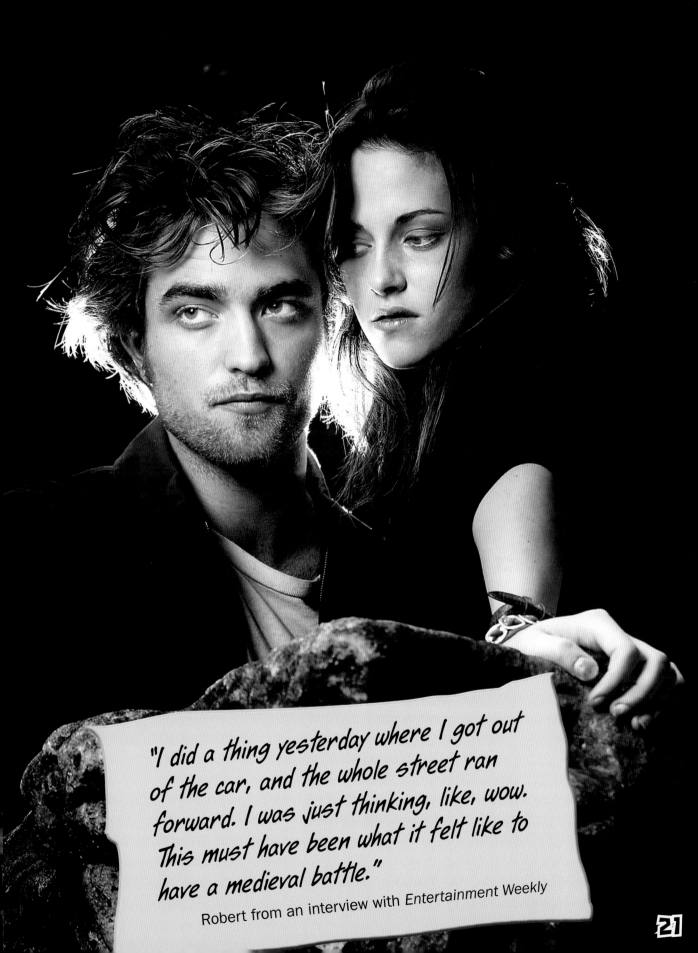

"I did a thing yesterday where I got out of the car, and the whole street ran forward. I was just thinking, like, wow. This must have been what it felt like to have a medieval battle."

Robert from an interview with Entertainment Weekly

Becoming a vampire

Robert took the role of Edward seriously. He worked hard to prepare for the part. For two months, Robert lived alone outside Portland, Oregon, in the United States, where the cast would shoot the film. To explore the **isolation** a vampire might feel, he didn't talk to anyone. Robert wrote journal articles from Edward's point of view. He went to the gym and ran every day to get in shape. He read and studied everything he could to connect with his character.

Robert also learned how to speak with an American accent. In his other roles, Robert's natural British accent had worked fine. He'd never attempted an American accent before. Robert watched films featuring US actors such as James Dean and John Wayne. He tried to copy the way they spoke. He figured out that if he got certain words right, such as 'water' and 'been', the rest would follow.

"I tried to make [Edward] into a real character, rather than just Dracula. A lot of the way Stephenie [Meyer] had written the books was trying to take vampires out of the world of cliche."

Robert from an interview with MTV

isolation being or feeling alone

 Robert and Kristen have good on-screen chemistry.

Lights, camera, action

Shooting the first Twilight film was both fun and frustrating for the actors. Every morning, Robert arrived on **set** at 5.45 a.m. Make-up artists turned his skin pale and styled his hair. Robert put in gold coloured contact lenses. For many of the scenes, the actors had to be rigged on wires. They soared through the air, and jumped through tree tops as they pretended to fight each other.

Fighting the weather became a daily task too. Oregon's weather seemed to change by the minute. It would rain, hail, and snow in a single day. Between scenes, the actors huddled under heaters in warm coats. On other days, the sun would shine. This was not good news. It delayed filming, because many Twilight characters are never seen in the sun. Through it all, Robert and his co-stars found plenty to laugh about. They grew to be good friends. And they all worked hard to make the best film they possibly could.

Robert's hard work and preparation paid off. When Twilight was released in November 2008, reviews raved about Robert's portrayal of Edward. Teenagers and adults flocked to cinemas to see the film. Twilight broke box office records around the world. Devoted fans – known as 'Twi-hards' – swarmed to see Robert in every city he visited. He had become a global superstar.

Twilight and its three sequels have sold more than 100 million copies.

From books to films

His roles in the *Harry Potter* and *Twilight* films made Robert Pattinson a household name. While the characters he plays are very different, the films do have one thing in common. They are both based on best-selling children's books.

The Twilight books have a huge fanbase, who speak to each other online. When Robert was cast as Edward Cullen, fans were furious. Internet message boards filled with complaints. They said the actor who played Cedric Diggory was not right for the part of Edward. People posted YouTube videos saying that Robert was too old and too ugly for the part. Almost 75,000 fans signed a petition demanding that Edward be recast.

Everything changed when the trailer for *Twilight* was released. All of a sudden, bloggers praised Robert in the role of Edward. *Twilight* fans gushed about the actor they had once rejected. Vanity Fair magazine has since voted Robert the Most Handsome Man in the World!

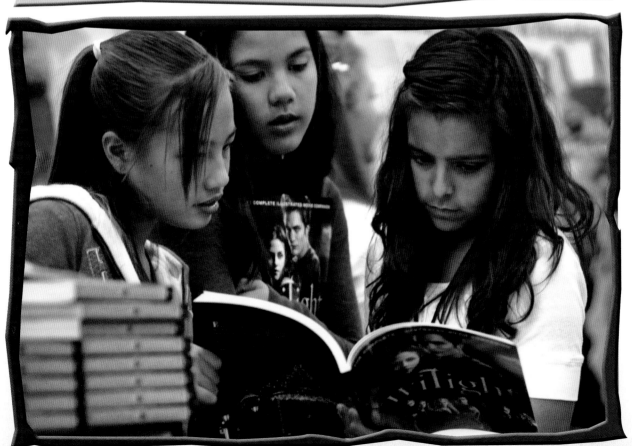

CHAPTER 5

A superstar in demand

Since the success of *Twilight*, Robert has been hot property. Fans can't get enough of him. Hollywood film-makers want him in their films. He's come a long way from his London school days. Now no one minds if he breaks the rules!

Robert returned to the role of Edward Cullen in *New Moon* (2009), *Eclipse* (2010) and *Breaking Dawn Parts 1 and 2* (2011 and 2012). Between them, the films in the Twilight Saga made more than £1 billion at the box office.

Robert didn't rest in his breaks between shooting the Twilight films. He took on several more starring roles. First he played the lead in the romantic drama *Remember Me* (2010). Robert also travelled to Hungary to film scenes in a film for his adult fans.

Robert worked with Reese Witherspoon again on *Water for Elephants* (2011). This time he was just as famous as Reese, and there was no risk that his scenes would be cut! Robert plays a student vet who joins a circus. He managed to keep his cool filming scenes where he fed real tigers.

Rob accepts the Global Superstar award at the MTV Movie Awards in 2010.

"It's probably one of the best experiences I've ever had making a movie .... I've been working with Reese [Witherspoon] for the last three days. She's amazing, great, funny."

Robert in 2011, on filming Water for Elephants

Never alone

Robert tries to lead a laidback lifestyle, but his fame makes privacy difficult. As soon as *Twilight* came out, rumours began that Robert was dating his co-star, Kristen. The pair kept the media and public guessing for years.

Paparazzi photographers follow Robert wherever he goes, waiting outside his homes in London and Los Angeles. They even come to film **sets**. On the set of *Water for Elephants*, photographers scared the animals and made it impossible to film. Robert was pleased when some fans, who were waiting for autographs, chased the paparazzi away.

A-list superstars need protection in case fans and photographers get a bit too excited. Up to 25 bodyguards look out for Robert at **premieres**. But stardom does come with some perks. Robert was paid £1.2 million for his performance in *Twilight*. This shot up to £7.6 million for the *Breaking Dawn* films, plus a share of the box office takings.

"I find periods to escape from it and places to get away as much as possible. I try and tell myself that it's just a job and that all this craziness won't last forever."

Robert on coping with the downsides of fame

paparazzi photographers who take pictures of celebrities, and sell them to magazines and newspapers

The future

Since filming the final scenes of the Twilight saga, Robert has worked harder than ever. He enjoys choosing challenging film roles, that help him 'realize something about himself'.

In a film for his adult fans Robert plays a billionaire on a strange journey through New York City. He is also working on new projects for his teenage fans. He even signed up to star in the Western *Unbound Captives*, because Westerns are his dad's favourite films.

Robert hopes that these diverse projects will develop his acting skills, and help him win an Oscar by the time he's 30.

Robert and co-stars Kristen Stewart and Taylor Lautner at the People's Choice awards in 2011.

Glossary

agent someone who helps actors to find work

audition a performance by an actor who is trying out for a role

epic a long story, poem, or film about heroic adventures and great battles

isolation feeling or being alone

paparazzi photographers who take unposed pictures of celebrities, and sell them to magazines and newspapers

premiere the first public performance of a film, play, or work of music or dance

prop items that are used by actors in a play or film

rebellious struggling against the people in charge

set the place where a film is shot, including the scenery and backgrounds

soundtrack the music from a film or play

suburb an area on the outskirts of a city

vintage from the past

Find out more

Books

10 Things You Need to Know About Being Famous, Jen Jones (Capstone Press, 2008)

Robert Pattinson A-Z, Sarah Oliver (John Blake, 2010)

The *Robert Pattinson Album*, Paul Stenning (Plexus, 2009)

Robert Pattinson Inside Out, Mel Williams (Piccadilly Press, 2008)

Websites

Get the latest R-Patz news, photos and gossip at his fansites, such as:
www.robert-pattinson.co.uk/

Fans of Robert as Edward Cullen will like the Twilight fan site **thetwilightsaga.com** and the official film website **www.twilightthemovie.com**

Find plots, photographs and quotes from Robert's latest film projects on his Internet Movie Database page:
www.imdb.com/name/nm1500155/

Index